# BUDGET BUCKS IN YOUR LAP

## Become a More Successful Whitetail Hunter Anywhere

### GALE ARDEN BOTT

STORY MERCHANT BOOKS
LOS ANGELES
2014

THE STORY MERCHANT

Budget Bucks in Your Lap

Facebook: Gale Bott

ISBN-13: 978-0-9904216-9-6
ISBN-10: 0-990-42169-4

Story Merchant Books
400 S. Burnside Ave. #11B
Los Angeles, CA 90036
http://www.storymerchant.com/books.html

Editor: Lisa Cerasoli
Cover: D. Bond Canfield
Interior Design: Lisa Cerasoli & Danielle Canfield

# BUDGET BUCKS IN YOUR LAP

### Become a More Successful
### Whitetail Hunter Anywhere

# Table of Contents

# A Note from the Author

This book began by accident in 2010. I was experimenting with making mock scrapes to see how effective they actually are. The area I used was Marquette County in Michigan's Upper Peninsula—thousands of pictures covering a large section of the county were accumulated in my experiment. The goal was based solely on my quest to become the best bow hunter I could be. The only animals I hunt are White-tailed deer. I'm totally fascinated with their habits and world. To me, there's not a more interesting animal on the planet. With their sudden surge in popularity over the past twenty or so years—because they are so cunning and curious—I'd say I'm not the only one who thinks that.

After testing different scent and lure combinations and documenting the results, it was time to share what was observed. The products and manufacturers mentioned throughout my manual were chosen because they flat out provided the best results. If you follow the technique developed the way it's explained in this book, nice bucks will visit your mock scrapes; I promise you that! Whether or not you get the opportunity to harvest one, well, that's up to you...even though I'd love to hunt with you.

Read this through in its entirety in order to get the full scoop as to why this is an amazing technique. I could be brief and just tell you how to use my mock scrape making technique—then show you a picture of a big buck—but it wouldn't do the entire process justice. Knowing why this method is so effective is half the excitement. Knowing where and when to use this technique will make you the envy of your hunting buddies. The more comfortable you become with this entire concept, the more confidence you'll have using it.

I've managed to record some excellent pictures of my technique in action—all the photos are time and date stamped for authenticity. The more confidence and understanding you have with my system, the more apt you are to implement it and teach others.

The research was conducted over a four year span in many different wilderness areas throughout the Upper Peninsula of Michigan. The photos throughout this manual are a select compilation chosen from between six and seven thousand game camera photographs. This system has proven itself over and over, but it won't work for you unless you have confidence in its ability to put nice bucks where you want them—in plain sight!

# My Deer Jargon

**Bait/feeding stations-** Mechanical devices used to disperse food onto the ground for the purpose of deer consumption. It can also be as simple as pouring food on the ground yourself in a certain area for immediate deer consumption, corn and carrots are examples.

**Buck-** A male White-tailed deer.

**Community scrape-** A type of scrape that is visited by multiple deer—bucks and does alike.

**Cook-** A term I use for giving a mock scrape time to let scent waft throughout the area and attract deer. The longer it's there, the better it will become.

**Core area-** An area where a buck spends the majority of his life.

**Decoy-** A replica of an actual deer, usually made out of some sort of foam.

**Deer Dander-** Small particles of skin and hair of deer, dandruff.

**Doe-** A female White-tailed deer.

**Eight-pointer-** A buck that has eight antler points.

**Estrus doe-** A doe that is ready to be bred by a buck. Their body releases a special hormone in their urine during this time of year.

**Food plots-** Areas that man has cultivated and planted food designed for deer consumption.

**Grunt call-** A manufactured device you inhale or exhale into with the desired effect of imitating the natural grunt sound a buck makes.

3

**Licking branch-** A branch that hangs directly over a scrape where deer deposit their scent.

**Mock scrape-** a manmade scrape used to imitate a natural one that a buck would make.

**Preorbital gland-** A scent gland located just in front of a deer's eye.

**Rattling-** The act of hitting deer antlers together to attract bucks. They can be either synthetic or real antlers.

**Runway-** A trail that deer follow through the woods.

**Rut-** The time of year when bucks are actively breeding does. In their Northern territories, it's early to mid-November.

**Scent dripper-** Store bought deer scent or lure containers used for the purpose of time releasing scent over a deer scrape.

**Scrape-** A term used for a patch of ground where a buck clears away the debris with his front legs to expose the dirt. Bucks and does alike deposit their scent in it through urination.

**Seven-pointer-** A buck that has seven antler points.

**Spike horn-** A buck with one antler point on each side of its head.

**Tarsal gland-** A scent gland located on the inside of a buck's legs that gets enlarged and becomes pungent smelling during the breeding season.

**Trail or game camera-** A camera designed to be put in the woods to monitor wildlife. The terms trail and game are interchangeable in this case.

# Simple System

To summarize this whole process and make it sound as simple as it actually is, I'll keep it brief. Everything will make sense as you read through the book. Explaining the process first will set the groundwork from which to build.

Find a likely spot for your mock scrape while keeping in mind all the variables I mention. Kick away the leaves and debris exposing the dirt in an area about the size of a truck tire. Then, spray the overhanging licking branch with "Deer Dander." Next, spray the scrape and surrounding area with "Deer Dander." Finally, apply "Buck Fever" synthetic deer urine directly on the scrape. Turn on your camera and leave—it's that simple!

**IMPORTANT:** Follow these steps (in this order) to mask your human scent because you will be spraying it after you've stepped in the scrape.

# The Joker on a Rope

It was a beautiful October evening in the Upper Peninsula of Michigan. All my senses were on high alert. I walked to my tree stand—adorned in full battle gear—in anticipation of the most incredible bow hunt of my life. I took in the prism of fall colors, noted the crunch of leaves under my boots and breathed in the freshest of all air and thought there's no other place I'd rather be! I first stopped at the mock scrape I'd created a week back to juice it up with my secret elixir, then turned and climbed a nearby tree and settled in for my first hunt at this spot.

Everything was visible from my perch high above the ground—atop a ridge, amongst a sea of open hardwoods. I wasn't alone—all of nature's majestic sights and sounds had joined me on this adventure. The night couldn't get any better...then I saw the buck. He walked across the logging road a few hundred yards away. I perched my binoculars on my nose. A seven-pointer was walking my way in broad daylight! I had just freshened up my mock scrape and was only in my tree stand about forty-five minutes as I watched this fine young buck go totally out of his way to climb the steep ridge to get to me. He was on the hunt for my mock scrape.

I could hardly contain myself. He was responding to something I'd done; this joker was coming to my scrape! He wasn't a monster buck by any means—nor did he have the look of the deer I'd imagined myself shooting the first time sitting it out near this mock scrape—but he was a nice young buck on a mission, drawn mystically to my handy work. I wasn't going to shoot him, so I did the next best thing—I started texting my best friend the play-by-play.

My wife (aka "my best friend") was with me when I found this spot a week earlier, so I texted her to let her in on this wonderful little secret as it was playing out right in front of me. I used to take her out in the woods as often as I could "research." These are just some of the memories that will never fade from my early experiments. She wasn't a hunter herself but like me, she loved nature and was intrigued by the peculiarities of deer.

The buck closed in as if being pulled on a rope like a minion in some trance-like state. He crested the top of the hill and strutted down the runway right up to my handy work. Then he stopped directly in front of the mock scrape—exactly where I hoped he would. He sniffed in and around it like a hound hot on a rabbit. I captured the moment on my cell phone and sent the photos to my wife at breakneck speed. Eventually, we both grew tired. He got bored with sniffing around and not finding his doe and my photos started blending together. He ultimately walked off, going about his business.

It finally dawned on me that my game camera was on the tree next to him filming the whole thing. I sat there in awe trying to figure out if what just happened really just happened…. Maybe I was hallucinating—half expecting to see blank images upon review; that seemed like a real possibility. But I viewed my cell phone pictures as soon as he

was clean out of sight. I wasn't crazy, after all. I had two dozen
pictures!

I started thinking of when we found that spot together. She said that I'd turn into a different person. I'd quit talking except to point out some extremely relevant deer stuff—evidence that sometime within the past century a deer passed through this certain area. I guess I also looked like a beagle running around with my nose to the ground on the scent of some critter. She'd say that other times I'd walk slowly with my head on a swivel looking up/down, left/right and so on. When she wasn't with me as a voice of reason, she knew the concept of time was lost on me. She was grateful for darkness…and my safe return.

Cell phones can really be a buzz kill when you've just found the most amazing deer area that man will ever see—a spot the likes of which none will ever compare. You can almost see the rainbow ending right there!

RING RING.

Urgh. "Hi honey, yes I'm leaving now."

Thank goodness most of my hunting areas don't have a cell phone signal.

## The Believer

That single event made me realize that my mock scrape technique actually worked and worked very well! I guess all the previous camera footage from different tests weren't enough; I had to witness it for myself in broad daylight from fifteen yards away to become a true believer. From that point on, I completely believed in my system. It will work for anyone as long as there are White-tailed deer in the woods. If you follow my technique, this system is foolproof.

# Close...but no Cigar

Later in that same month, I was sitting in a tree stand about sixty yards from a different scrape I'd made. I was out of bow range but was there trying to figure out where the bucks went after they left the scrape. It was breaking daylight, and I could only see about thirty yards out. Beyond that, I needed my binoculars to see whether or not a deer had antlers. I was feeling a bit cocky and confident that this hot scrape would pull them in like a magnet. I'll never forget whispering, "I bet there's a nice buck on my scrape right now," as I slowly pulled my binoculars to my eyes. I about fell out of my tree when I saw a tall tined eight-pointer "stamped" to the lenses of my binoculars. He was exactly where I had imagined him to be. This story doesn't end as cool as the last one though. Either me, or the tree I was in moved too much—he vanished and gave me the slip. I'm forever hooked on my mock scrape system, and I get excited at the thought of all the new stories and White-tailed encounters to come. Sharing what I've learned is exciting because every hunter can experience wonderful memories like these while afield.

# The Licking Branch

The "licking branch" portion of making a mock scrape is crucial, and my method needs to be adhered to in order to pull off this magic trick. **The licking branch is the single most important component of a scrape, either mock or real.** To look natural, the licking branch has to be sticking out over your mock scrape at about eye level, or just a little higher.

Spray the licking branch above your scrape liberally with "Deer Dander"—to the point of being able to see it pooling up on the underside of the overhanging branch. (More about "Deer Dander" later.) If there are several branches on the same overhanging limb, spray them also. If the scent is on other branches overhanging very close to the chosen one, deer in general respond more favorably—they would naturally leave their scent on them also.

On one particular scrape, there was a maple leaf hanging off the end of the licking branch. I sprayed that leaf liberally also and got some nice results. The deer kept batting it around with their noses and heads—rubbing their scent on it.

Based on the footage, every deer that visited that particular scrape messed around with the hanging leaf and put their scent on it. If there are no leaves on your chosen branch, add one! If the branch you've found is perfect, add a leaf or two to it by poking them onto the branch, and spray it with Deer Dander. The leaves will hang there looking

14

natural, dispersing scent, no worries. You also eliminate the expense of buying a hanging scent wick that manufacturers advertise. Other hunters will also see a scent wick hanging there—you don't want others messing around in your mock scrape area.

# Community Scrapes

A buck makes scrapes in the fall in hopes of luring receptive female deer (does) into his trap. Other bucks will visit the scrape he's made in hopes of catching the scent of a receptive doe to breed also.

A scrape is simply a small patch of ground that has all the debris and leaves kicked away to expose the dirt. It's a natural phenomenon in their world. The scrape's sole purpose is to lure does in for breeding. Whether this is a learned behavior or an instinctual one, has been long up for debate. The only thing we know for sure is that this scraping activity is effective.

We, as hunters, have the opportunity to use this lovesick weakness to our advantage. I have many documented pictures of multiple bucks using the same scrapes I've made. **Not just one or a few scrapes, rather, almost all became community scrapes if my mock scrape method was adhered to properly.** All the age classes of bucks will be represented at each site without fail. Just like with humans, bucks are just "boys looking for girls." And, just like with humans, the does show up because they're curious to see who the eligible bachelors are in the area. A mock scrape can be a very effective tool in harvesting a nice buck. It can also be a very simple and inexpensive process if you follow my field-researched and tested method.

# Truck Tire

Make your scrapes about the size of a truck tire (that's a good way to remember the size). When you make a scrape, try to make it from one specific spot and push the dirt in one direction like a buck would do. You want it to look and smell natural. Bucks will generally stand in one spot and kick the dirt behind them with their front leg, so mimic that movement with your boot. As mentioned earlier, this dirt that's kicked behind the scrape should be sprayed with Deer Dander, to make it more realistic. Always try to keep it simple and natural.

I prefer to use my boots because they do a nice job in working up the soil quickly. **Remember, you always have to have an overhanging licking branch above your mock scrape! This must also be sprayed with Deer Dander for the system to work.**

You don't need to get all crazy with scent elimination—with the added expense in making sure there is zero human scent on your boots. The Deer Dander and Buck Fever lures do a nice job of masking your scent anyway (more on these two products later). In fact, on occasion, my hound dog has been known to run through and smell my scrapes while I'm making them because he's curious too! Bucks and does still visit it, often the same day.

On public land, deer are used to human and dog odor as long as it isn't frequent. Think about it, if deer were spooked by every human and pet smell, we would have no deer anywhere because humans and dogs have explored almost every inch of our public land. With that said, I have no footage of any deer ever getting spooked and taking off after smelling a scrape that I made, whether my dog was with me or not (except one time which I will explain later).

# Michigan's Upper Peninsula...or Anywhere

The areas used exclusively for these experiments were all in the big woods of Michigan's Upper Peninsula in Marquette County. As the name implies, it is just that—huge sections of wilderness. There are no crop fields or food plots. Every area chosen was open to public hunting. **My method is designed for anybody to use effectively anywhere!** With this said, one can also deduce that some pre-scouting would need to be done to find natural feeding and bedding areas.

Bow hunting has been my passion for over thirty years, and I've gathered vast amounts of information in relation to how deer operate. I could honestly ramble on and on about deer behaviors and habits. My goal here is to share field tested information that will literally put Bucks in Your Lap in a simple and inexpensive way!

The easiest way to get started in a new area is to wander the woods giving it a quick overview. Look for deer sign and get an understanding of the terrain. Look for terrain breaks that may funnel deer through a certain area. Look for water, food, and bedding areas. Fresh deer scat is another good clue that they've been around. Areas of thick cover with easy access to a food source are excellent also. Once you find a deer "runway," you're in business. When you find a buck rub or two in the area, you know for a fact that there is at least one buck in the area. When you're making mock scrapes, the size of the rubs in the area (or even their presence) isn't crucial at this point. The bigger bucks will make their presence known because they're bullies! But, the closer you can get to a bigger buck's bedding area, the better your chances will be at a shot during legal shooting hours.

This system is easy and affordable for any hunter to incorporate into his bag of tricks, and you'll have the opportunity to shoot or film a nice buck. To keep it simple and brief, a nice buck is a relative term used to describe a buck that's dominant or mature in your area. One of the bigger bucks in your area is considered a nice buck, because every area is different. The mature bucks in your area will visit your scrapes guaranteed!

Some areas contain food plots, crop fields and or bait/feeding stations that play a role in antler growth. The areas chosen contain none of the above mentioned variables. These areas have had no added outside nutrition, just what nature already offers. These experiments serve as a baseline test, the more positive variables you add, the better your results.

An added bonus of making your own scrapes—and hopefully placing trail cameras on them—is that it's also a lot of fun watching bucks on film coming to visit. This is an activity even the non-hunter will enjoy.

# Keep Them Apart

Even though it's fun viewing footage, take heed in not making too many scrapes in one area. Doing so creates too many places to hunt and increases the chance of a nice buck slipping past you undetected. Keep it to one or two scrapes that you can effectively hunt with favorable wind conditions for that given day. If you want to make several scrapes, keep them far away from each other—the further the better. You don't want the same bucks visiting multiple scrapes in the area; it makes patterning them too difficult.

If you make mock scrapes less than a quarter of a mile away from each other, you'll get pictures of the same bucks visiting the different scrapes because their territories overlap. A lot of educated people with pockets full of degrees who spend their entire lives researching White-tailed deer re-sound the same message: bucks will live and die within a quarter square mile area. This is called their "core area." Because of this fact, these core areas overlap. Finding these "buck core areas" is a good thing for a hunter. If you're lucky enough to accidentally put a mock scrape in an overlapping core area, you'll know it because it'll quickly become a hot scrape guaranteed. Bucks leave their core area when they're in search of does for breeding purposes. This area expands the more they search for receptive does during the breeding season. They'll look just about anywhere for the right girl. You'll be making your scrapes before the breeding season. Therefore, the bucks will generally still be in their core areas. This is the time you want to harvest a nice buck, while he's still home instead of out carousing. You know where he's at for now!

# Maximize Your Time on Stand

Your mock scrapes are basically giving you a census of the different bucks that are in the area. With that said, by keeping them further than a quarter mile away from each other, you can get a sample of different bucks in different areas. Find other areas, even miles away to put mock scrapes. The more you make, the better your chances of finding the biggest buck become——as long as they aren't too close to each other. It also greatly increases your chances of finding overlapping core areas. You'll discover that some deer are very active and responsive to your scrapes in certain areas. Spend your time and hunting efforts around the hot scrape areas.

This makes your time on stand more exciting because you know what lurks there. The areas that have more hunting pressure or lack of sustainable food sources will be crossed off your list for that season. The next season may be an entirely different ballgame. Tuck these "notes" away in your memory. **It's all about maximizing your time on stand this season!**

# Quick and Easy

We've all watched hunting shows that demonstrate how to make an effective mock scrape. You know as well as I do that if we do it the way the so-called experts describe, we'll be spending a lot of money on specialized scents or lures. Deer use different glands to leave their scent on a scrape. The preorbital and forehead gland lures are for the licking branch. The Tarsal gland lure and the Estrus doe urine lure are for the ground.

Each one of these highly specialized scents can cost in excess of $15 per bottle. Lastly, to do it the way "the experts" suggest, you need to buy special scent-activated dirt to add to the natural dirt that's already there to hold the pricey scent lure you apply. It sounds silly to me—adding dirt to dirt!

Manufacturers and hunting professionals also want you to wear waders or rubber hip boots and shoulder high rubber gloves to further mask our human scent. I wonder if these people want us to look silly just so they can chuckle at the thought of us wandering around in the woods looking as if we're cleaning up a nuclear spill. They say we have to dress that way to trick a deer…. Who is actually being tricked here?

After adding up the cost of all this stuff, you can easily spend over $100, not to mention the hassle of lugging all of that gear into the woods—in your hot rubber space suit—for the sole purpose of making mock scrapes. If this sounds like too much of an ordeal to undertake, it's because it is!

**My system makes hunting more enjoyable and less expensive for anyone!** You only need to carry two bottles of inexpensive lures into the woods. They easily fit in your pockets, (my method doesn't require a space suit). Another cost saving bonus is that these lures are not specialized and can be used to increase your chances at harvesting a nice buck in your everyday hunting adventures as well. They're not designed solely for scrape hunting. The best part is that you can make a scrape quickly—whenever you want—and you'll always have your two lures with you (not wasting any of your valuable, ever shrinking free time).

# Make it and Let it Cook

Make your scrapes and let them "cook." Letting the scrape cook is key to its simplistic effectiveness. When you arouse a deer's curiosity to the point that it deposits its own scent—by rubbing its scent on the licking branch and/or depositing its scent in the scrape through urination—it now becomes a natural or active scrape. The more deer that deposit their scent, the more effective it will be, soon making it more arousing to nice bucks.

The biggest question is how to do this effectively with minimal expense and effort. As I mentioned before, I use only two attractants in the making of my scrapes. Because everyone's time is so important, a general rule is that the nicer bucks start showing up between the first and second week. You can hunt them right away, even that same day if you like. But since maximizing your chance of shooting a nice buck is the goal, wait at least a week or more before you start hunting your scrapes. With that said, generally the smaller bucks and does will visit it first. As a general rule, except for overlapping core areas, my scrapes "cooked" for at least a week or more before the bigger bucks started showing up. Mock scrapes become more effective for bigger bucks when there's scent from multiple deer in it. When your scrape has been there for a little while, it'll become a community scrape. Different deer will cruise through to check for activity, thus leaving their scent also. You can't count on every scrape you make to magically be

26

in overlapping core areas though. Letting them cook will lure the nicer bucks in, guaranteed! **It's important to remember that right after the first buck places his scent on your scrape, it's now a natural scrape.**

I will go so far in saying that if you clear away the dirt in an area to make it look like a scrape, a buck or doe that walks within eyesight of it will investigate out of instinct and curiosity. But in order for a deer to actually believe it's a scrape, there has to be an overhanging branch above it. That's an absolute requirement for any scrape, natural or homemade (mock). The overhanging branch often referred to, as "the licking branch" is where deer also deposit their scent. Deer will walk through it without the scented licking branch present and likely pause to smell the scrape, but they will NOT be actively engaged, and it will NOT become a community scrape!

# Make Your Scrapes Early

Misnomer: Deer will only respond to scrapes just before, during, or just after the rut. Bucks and does respond to mock scrapes before bow season even opens, **(October 1st in the North)** several weeks to a month before the rut starts.

Get your scrapes made early. Shortly after they shed their velvet is best, so you'll have a clear idea of which areas have the biggest bucks to target for that hunting season. Start making your scrapes a few days to a week before the opening of bow season, October 1st in the North. This allows the scrapes time to cook before you hunt them. Letting your scrapes cook is key to its effectiveness. You will have seen enough of the bigger bucks on camera before the rut is in full swing (before they leave the area in search of receptive does) to determine which scrapes to target.

You will have a nice buck visiting your scrape early in the season, but then he'll vanish during the breeding season. This is why you want to make them early and let them cook. It gives you enough time to find the one you want to pursue before they get lovesick and leave.

An interesting discovery was that when the rut was on and in full swing, the nicer bucks and does visited the scrapes far less than they did earlier in the season. This is attributed to an increase in the radius of their roaming activity, and because bucks intercept receptive does before they make it to the scrapes. This is an excellent time to use your rattling horns to possibly harvest a nicer buck cruising for does. Rattling is a hot topic that will be discussed in the near future.

As a general rule once again, a week or two before the bucks are in search of receptive does for breeding, the nicer bucks showed up on my mock scrapes. One thing that's consistent with the research is that smaller bucks show up first and within a week or two, the nicer ones follow guaranteed! Once the scrape has become established—or

31

turned into a community one—the bucks visit it in no particular order, randomly visiting. In some areas, there were no smaller bucks, just nicer ones. Oh, darn!

The series of photos that follow were taken for my cousin. We share a mutual passion for deer hunting. A few years back he harvested the second largest buck recorded with archery equipment in Marquette County. He loves the outdoors so much that he makes his living as one of the managers of a national outdoor company.

One day I was telling him about the mock scrape technique I had stumbled upon and how reliable and amazing it was. His reaction was typical of most hunters. "They don't work very well," and "they're too much of a hassle."

I told him that there's a nice 100+ acre chunk of public land nearby that we should hunt.

I had my "inside guy" download the satellite imagery with landowner boundaries on Google Earth Map. He downloaded the GPS coordinates for tree stand and mock scrape locations also. Everything I was hoping for was well within public hunting areas. My cousin saw the area on the map and said he used to hunt there but gave up on it because there weren't any bucks around. I'm telling you my technique will still work! I didn't want to argue with him—I wanted to prove him wrong.

"The winters get so harsh that all the deer migrate out to avoid certain death, and to make things worse, there are a lot of guys hunting in there and the deer don't seem to be around." Those were some of his complaints, I knew I had a big task ahead of me.

"I'll put some mock scrapes back in there and I guarantee you we'll get nice bucks on camera!"

Extreme skepticism was the prevailing look on his face.

Even though an avid hunter proclaimed the absence of deer in that area and threw in harsh winters and extreme hunting pressure to boot—I still believed it would work; my confidence didn't waiver. The next series of pictures came from one mock scrape in this area that was thought to be void of bucks. He was amazed and had no answer for what he saw. Not only was there a nice eight-pointer standing right on the scrape, but his eight point buddy was in the background checking things out.

There were at least six different bucks on that exact scrape. Believe in it and just do it! It will work anywhere. **These images also prove once again that bucks will visit a scrape before deer season even opens.**

Later that season we were hunting together somewhere else on a little oak ridge hot spot. Our hunt was over for the morning. My cousin walked through the hardwoods in my direction to gather me up so we could walk out to base camp together. He stopped about sixty yards away from my tree and was up to something, but I couldn't quite see what he was doing. I started packing up my gear figuring he was heading my way. A few minutes passed and the familiar sound of shuffling leaves made me think he was at my tree. I looked up from what I was doing and saw a beautiful young four-pointer right in front of me. He was maybe ten yards away just messing around in the leaves, making a ruckus. He sure didn't look like my cousin. It took a minute of head scratching to process that one. He was tall and wide, but it was his lucky day. He was the biggest four-pointer I'd ever seen, but I wasn't going to harvest that young buck.

Back at the truck, my cousin asked if I'd seen any deer. *Are you kidding me? That buck must've walked right passed you.* He said he didn't see the buck because he must have been making a mock scrape at the time. That brought a smile to my face. Seeing the buck in that situation wasn't the cool thing, it was hearing my cousin say he was making a mock scrape. He's becoming more of a believer in mock scrape magic every day.

# The White Hound and the Hot Scrape

Don't be surprised if an area you suspect of having few bucks magically produce several thanks to your scrape (you'll see for yourself when you review your camera footage). You'll notice other natural scrapes and rubs pop up in the area after you've made your mock scrape. Your camera footage will help determine which scrapes to focus on during your hunt and which to consider your hot scrapes.

The following pictures are a brief sample taken from one of my hot scrapes. I was with my wife and hound when it was made. Our hound was exceptionally untamed that day. He even had to stop and sniff the scrape to make sure I did it right. I chuckled and thought that there was no way I'd get any usable deer footage after we stunk up the place. But I had gotten pictures of several smaller bucks and does visiting it that first week and knew it had potential. On my way to hunt a different tree stand one evening, I swung by to freshen up this scrape with my scent lures (every five days is sufficient). You don't want to visit your scrape too often, leaving a constant scent trail. I was in the area that day and stopped by to give it a little extra magic, nonetheless.

About five days after that visit, my wife and I went back and pulled the SD card from the camera. We were speechless. All of the scrapes I had made were in the desolate North Woods of Michigan's Upper Peninsula. In a fifteen minute time span, four different bucks showed up at this scrape during legal shooting hours. Multiple buck sightings are not a common occurrence. We weren't supposed to be seeing this kind of stuff up here, I thought. But here we were, sitting on the hottest scrape around. At least eight different bucks had visited that one particular scrape.

## Greedy

Knowing what you have in the area is a dual edged sword. We all tend to get a bit greedy and want to shoot the biggest, baddest buck we see on our game cameras. It happened to me in 2010. I got greedy and ended up with nothing but a large helping of hoof soup. In the previous picture (2010-10-14 7:47:37), a nice eight-pointer's standing behind the dandy that's posing for the camera. Of course, the bigger one was on my menu, and because of it, I got a taste of hoof soup. I rattled in the smaller of the two bucks one morning, but greed did me in.

# Rattling

Horn rattling is very similar to my mock scrape method. **You have to believe in it for it to work.** If you don't believe in it, you're going to go about it haphazardly and fidget in your stand. If you fidget or move around too much on stand, the jigs up and the buck will vanish before you even see him. For every one buck you see, there are several you don't! You have to have the mindset that every time you rattle, bucks will respond.

I had no intention of discussing rattling techniques in this book because it's about mock scrapes, but I had a great photo and story of the nice buck above. The art of rattling is just that, it's an art and deserves the respect or attention to detail any art deserves. Too many people aren't sure how to do it, so they give up because they don't get results. Rattling in a buck is an extreme rush; everyone should experience it. It's actually quite simple and very effective if done properly. Will it work every time? No. Will it work on every buck? No. It's another tool to put in your hunting arsenal, alongside mock scrapes when the situation calls for it. These techniques will help you become a more successful and well-rounded hunter. **Scrape hunting becomes less effective in general as the rut approaches, and horn rattling becomes more effective.** They go hand-in-hand. Therefore, the art of rattling needs to be addressed to give it the credit it deserves.

44

We've all poured over countless hunting videos and read more hunting articles than we care to remember. We don't often hear hunters talk in detail about how they rattle. A lot of people that rattle don't have an actual system or practiced technique that consistently works. You can just go out there and bang horns together and hope it works if you want. You can also read from someone that's had plenty of success and developed a system with confidence. Just like anything else in hunting and life, if you're going to do something, learn how to do it in a way that produces the best results for you. Too many people don't think it works or think it only rarely works. If this happens, you need to stop and think why that is. It's not that it isn't effective. Maybe you need to change how you're doing it. Einstein defines Insanity as: *"doing the same thing over and over expecting different results."* Anybody can be successful at it with a little guidance. I use the exact same strategy every time. I've rattled in many bucks of all age classes.

The smaller ones approach very cautiously because they've had their butts kicked by bigger bucks before. They are the ones you have to be careful of (more on that later). The bigger, more dominant ones come in less cautiously. The smaller ones come out of curiosity to watch the schoolyard fight, purely as spectators. The bigger ones have a different agenda; they're more like the school bully who comes to the show because someone else is on his turf. Before you even see his antlers, his body language will be a dead giveaway to his status in the neighborhood herd. The subordinate bucks tend to sneak in making little noise. They survey the scene very carefully, and it seems every step is calculated. You would too if you'd already been kicked around and beat up more times than you care to remember. Even the poor little bucks try to keep their dignity if possible. The bigger bucks tend to be more fueled by aggression, so they make mistakes. A lot of the time you'll catch their careless movement or hear them coming.

It's the little buck that's our nemesis. You have to be careful not to spook them when they arrive. They'll spot your movements if you're not careful, always keep that in mind. If you do this, you'll soon become accustomed to always being cautious while on stand rattling. For every buck you see while rattling, there are several that you don't see. If you spook a smaller buck, it will clear the area of anything else bigger lurking. You still always have to be cautious of your movement, but as a general rule, the larger ones are a bit more tolerant. Error on the side of caution and restrict your movement when rattling.

Try to rattle the same way every time in every situation. Use a rattling sequence containing three different rattling sessions. Each session should last between forty-five seconds to a minute with roughly a two minute pause in between. It helps to put yourself in the deer's hooves, so to speak. It gives you a better appreciation for the whole process. Try to think of what's going through mister bucks mind, it will help you restrict your movement.

Before you start rattling, survey the area with your binoculars. Next, use your grunt call in a series of three short grunts like this:

"Grunt," I exhale once with a momentary pause before adding, "grunt, grunt."

Then check for deer using your optics again. Only when you're sure nothing's close, start your first session of rattling. This should be fairly quiet to start. You do this because if there happens to be a buck within earshot that's hidden, he'll respond without getting startled. If he's fairly close and you bang the horns together loudly, he'll take off, and hoof soup will be on the menu!

After you've rattled, pause and use your grunt call now as previously demonstrated. Use you call sparingly though, and only do it a few different times during the pause. If nothing shows up while you're constantly keeping your movements to a minimum, start your second session.

The second session is by far the loudest. You know nothing is close enough to spook because you've already surveyed your area carefully. You're trying to make the bucks think there's a serious fight off in the distance over a girl that they just have to come check out. With this series, not only are you banging the horns together, you're also grinding them together. Picture two bucks locked in combat, their horns pressed tight, interwoven, and grinding back and forth. Try to emulate that. It's like the first session but on steroids. With the first session, you tick the antler tines together more lightly. If you do grind them in the first, do it softly. If nothing shows up after you pause and use your grunt call, start your last session—but only after you're sure nothing's in the area.

The last session is quiet again like the first. Imagine the buck's heading your way but you can't quite see him yet. You now rattle softly so he doesn't get spooked because he's closer and knows exactly where you are! You can almost see him strutting. When you're done rattling, use your grunt call again. When that's over, sit tight, scan the area, and wait. This is when you'll see the majority of the bucks slipping in. Between fifteen and twenty-five minutes after you're done rattling is when you'll most likely have action. This is the most crucial time, so you have to have all your wits about you. Too many people don't give it long enough. Sometimes they start moving around in frustration. Bucks don't come running in announcing, "Here I am!" Patience is key. Grunt every few minutes or so for at least thirty minutes after you're done rattling before you give up on it for the day. The buck is close by and knows exactly where the fight should have been but doesn't see anything. If you continue to use your grunt call undetected, he'll be reassured and come your way. They're masters at knowing exactly where sounds come from because their lives depend on it! When they come in, they'll come literally to your tree!

It was early November and the bucks weren't visiting my scrapes as often. Perched in a tree about sixty yards away from that mock scrape, a different strategy was on the docket for the day. Horn rattling can be lethal that time of year, that was the agenda for that beautiful, crisp November 3rd morning. When the sun starts to shine above the ridge tops, the bucks become more active, especially that time of year—

which makes it an opportune time to rattle. A lot of the time it seems my buck encounters happen in the morning. It was about 9:15 a.m., and I knew the bucks were feeling frisky. About two hundred yards in front of me, the two nice bucks previously pictured (2010-10-14 7:47:37), stepped into an opening. They were majestic; the bigger one was raking trees with his antlers and the smaller one just hung out. He knew if he started rubbing trees with his bigger buddy there, a losing fight would surely be the result. It was stressful trying to keep track of who's who from my tree stand. The sun was shining off their horns making them both look huge! Of course, my binoculars made them look even bigger. The mock scrape was between us, but they started to head in a different direction looking for the does that had just passed through. After they were out of sight, I gave it about five minutes before I executed my usual rattling routine. About fifteen minutes after I'd finished, I heard a branch break behind me. I knew it was a buck because I'd continued grunting after I'd rattled. I slowly looked back and at about twenty five yards directly behind me, at a real scrape, (they copied mine) stood a nice eight-pointer. I studied him long and hard. He was beautiful with all the tines of his rack tipping inward. I swear the top inch of each dagger like tine, was a shiny white. He was majestic and proud as he pranced around in the wide open creek bed. The mind races at times like this. *My bow hunting vacation hadn't even started yet. If I take this buck, I wouldn't have the thrill of hunting this area anymore. Where the heck is his buddy? Did he intercept one of those does? Is he right behind me somewhere? Where's the bigger one?*

Even though we are allowed to shoot two bucks in Michigan, I only shoot one per hunting area. The biggest reason why he escaped a dismal fate that morning was because the "greedy horn hunter" in the tree above him knew he had a bigger buddy in the area. Even though this buck looked so much bigger and more majestic in person than he did on camera, I knew he had to be the smaller of the two—and greed did me in. I got my money's worth that morning and messed around with my grunt call to bring him back a few times after he left though. I figured I might as well practice my grunting technique on him.

Cameras can be our downfall. Most people, myself included, would have been tickled pink to harvest that buck that was rattled in that morning. Hunters sometimes have to take what they're given. I didn't shoot the bigger one that year, nor did I harvest the smaller one for that matter. Hindsight's 20/20! Any decent buck you rattle in—or that comes to your mock scrape on public land—is a trophy worthy of serious consideration.

As a side note, I was at that exact same mock scrape in August 2013. It was 2010 when I made that scrape, and it was still there. It became a community scrape like a lot of them become, and will be there year after year. They took over my mock scrape and claimed it as their own; I'm okay with that.

# Big Brother Didn't Know Back Then

Many years ago, my big brother Thom and I were bow hunting this prime farmland in Lower Michigan. He was about 80 yards upwind of me and wanted to rattle in a buck for his little brother. Ten minutes after he was done, a four-pointer came within 30 yards of me, wandered around for a bit, then left. A few minutes later, a six-pointer showed up and did the same thing. They really wanted to get closer to the action. They kept looking in my brother's direction but got discouraged or became uninterested and eventually walked off. A few minutes later a big ten-pointer cut across the corner of the hay field and into the wooded lot in front of me. He was within range but needed to come a few steps closer for a clear shot. He did the same thing the other two did and just walked off. I wish I'd had a two way radio back then— "Thom hit your grunt call, the bucks are hanging up back here." Needless to say, I was shot from the excitement and couldn't wait to tell him the news. Ironically, he didn't see anything because he didn't continue using his grunt call to coax them closer.

He had three different bucks 100 yards away and had no clue. Think like a deer, and you'll be more successful at this technique also. **Bucks respond to rattling every time, they're just not always visible.** This is the mindset you always have to have.

There are lots of different kinds of rattling horns on the market. The ones that work best for me are made of wood dowels in a cloth bag. The longer dowels seem to have a more natural pitch and tone. The shorter and easier to transport ones work alright, but I have total confidence in the longer version. Real horns and synthetic horns work well also but are quite bulky and cumbersome to tote around. Spend the day just roaming around rattling. If you're a Turkey hunter, wear your turkey hunting vest with hunter orange and throw the big synthetics in the pouch. Hunker down by a tree and rattle. If nothing shows up after half an hour, move 300 or 400 yards away and start over. You can spend the day enjoying the woods doing that. You may even run into a nice buck in the process.

# Oops

It was the sixth day of rifle season in Michigan's Upper Peninsula, and I hadn't hunted yet. I shot a nice drop-tined nine-pointer with my bow just before rifle season opened and was busy getting that ready to take to the taxidermist. I was still in total bow hunting mode that morning. I grabbed my synthetic horns and off to the deer woods I went. There was a dominant buck I was after that was too stubborn to come to my mock scrape during legal shooting hours. That morning, I was going to slip in there and try to rattle him in.

The sun was peaking above the trees and started to warm things up, but it was still a brisk November morning in the North woods. About fifteen minutes after the banging was over, he came. There was no doubt he was the dominant buck I was after. He came strutting along a hardwood ridge that was adjacent to me about 80 yards out. He was neither happy nor shy as he came in from my right scraping the ground and raking trees along that ridge in an effort to get to me. When I hit the grunt call, he would stop and rake some trees with his horns and kick up dirt. We played this little game the whole length of the ridge on his quest to dominate me. He now only had to come 30 or 40 yards closer for an easy bow shot. The buck I had been after that entire bow season was before me—a big mature ten-pointer. He was about to have a bad day. I was hunkered down behind a log jam and reached down to grab my bow, oops—my RIFLE. Crap! I could've shot him a hundred times already. The big buck had already started to circle downwind of me to catch my scent. He slipped into the thick stuff. Had I had my wits about me instead of getting all stupid goofy over this majestic buck, he would've been my trophy. It was too late for a clean shot when I got my gun up and ready. I don't regret that ending for a second because I love messing with deer. Watching him carrying on like that is why I love hunting. I tricked him; that's what mattered to me.

# Rattle the Beast's Cage

Every mock scrape had at least one or two nice bucks visit it during shooting hours. Once again, the tests were conducted in tough hunting areas where buck sign is limited at best without the use of mock scrapes. If you hunt an area with a better buck-to-doe ratio, or an area rich with food plots and or farm fields, your results will be even better.

There are also things that you can do to elicit aggression and incite competition within the bucks in your area. An example would be to make a scrape next to an existing one that a buck already made. The trick is to make it slightly bigger than the natural one. The buck that made the original scrape will feel the competition and come check it out.

The next series of pictures come with a unique story. There was an existing natural scrape by a runway. To rile the beast that made it, I made a bigger one next to his. The first two deer depicted are coming by to check out the new guy on the block. You can tell by their posture they're just curious. The last buck on the scene is the cat that made the original mock scrape. It's obvious by his aggressive posture and straight back tail that he wasn't there to play nice. He displayed the classic body language of a dominant buck ready to breed and felt the threat of a potential rival in the area. He wasn't a monster buck by any means, but mature and dominant. He was a prime candidate for rattling.

Put a stand up sixty yards or so from that scrape with a wind direction to keep you hidden from his nose, and you can almost guarantee a magical hunt. The smaller bucks in the area came to investigate and left their scent, effectively making it a natural/community scrape. You can harvest any of the three bucks that showed up at the scrape, but their posture gives away their status in the local herd. If you want to wait for the mature one, by all means wait. It's your scrape and your hunt.

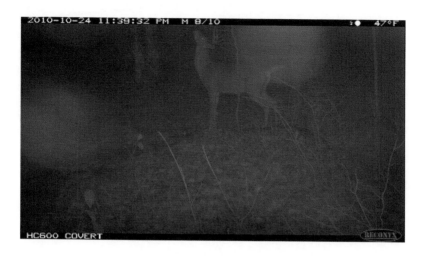

Another way to elicit excitement is to make your scrape next to an active runway. Employ this tactic whenever possible and seek out natural deer runs when looking for a place to make a scrape. Make it about two feet off the runway with an overhead licking branch and suitable tree stand location close by.

Don't put your scrape too close to—or on their—natural travel way...because that would not be natural. It makes sense from a buck's perspective that if a scrape were on a deer runway, every deer would leave their scent, and that's too confusing. On the other hand, if his scrape were a few feet off of a deer runway, only the more receptive does will walk through it, making less work for his nose.

# A Decent Buck with no Deer Sign

I did a test in an area sought out that was totally void of any deer sign from my perspective. I did this test to see just how long it took deer, especially bucks to show up, and to see if they would at all. Nothing showed up for a few days. A few does checked it out first, then a day or two after that a spike horn investigated the scrape. It took longer for a nicer buck to show up, around the second week. In my opinion, does and a smaller buck had to visit the scrape first to make it interesting enough to a nicer buck.

# Deer Sign Equals Deer

The interesting thing was that even though the nicer buck came to the scrape well before dark, he was only on camera one evening. He had been there more than once because there was another scrape and some rubs made outside of the camera's periphery. The chance of seeing him there again wasn't high enough to warrant hanging a tree stand. To maximize your chance of seeing a nicer buck to shoot, put your scrape near an active deer runway. The more deer sign you have in any given area, the more bucks you'll attract. They will show up sooner and return more often.

If you're making mock scrapes for hunting purposes—and not merely to study deer in their natural habitat—keep in mind tree stand locations when determining a good spot to mess with the dirt. You always have to be conscious of a likely tree stand location with favorable wind conditions for each scrape location. Put your stand with a wind direction that's blowing away from where you think the buck will be coming. Don't let your wind blow toward the scrape either. Remember this when deciding where to make your scrape.

# Scents/Lures

There are cost effective scents, for those of us on a budget that can be used the entire season (not just for the purposes of making mock scrapes). It's a very simple concept that even we hunters can understand. One lure smells like deer, and the other smells like its pee. These smells are related to all deer, not to just one particular deer that may or may not live in the same zip code. They'll be less weary and more curious this way, with these generic scents. Therefore, deer smell and deer pee got the nod! The ones I chose smell like every deer, any deer.

One or the other alone will not produce the desired results. You need to use them both in the manner I recommend, no exceptions. Many manufacturers sell scents that smell like deer, and likewise there are different manufacturers that sell the type of urine I chose, synthetic. Through trial and error, I ultimately settled on the formulas that gave me the best results plain and simple. If you try different formulas that accomplish the same goal—of smelling authentically like the odor of a deer and its urine—stick to your scents. Use it the way I recommend, or it will not work.

I use a deer scent from "Team Fitzgerald," called Deer Dander. I chose Deer Dander because it smells like the essence of deer (dander). What a deer smells like if you walk up to it and smell it's hide—that's the best way to describe the odor. The Deer Dander scent has a calming effect in that the smell convinces deer that other deer have frequented the area recently.

This is the only lure you put on the licking branch. It doesn't contain the same ingredients as the Pre-orbital or forehead gland lures that you can buy at a premium price. It works just as effectively and is much cheaper and easier to obtain. The "Deer Dander" I use is a four ounce version costing between $10-$15. This deer dander product is unique in the way it dispenses the scent. There are other manufactures that produce a similar deer dander type of lure but these use a deodorant type of roll on applicator or a hardened gel. Team Fitzgerald's "Deer Dander" is unique in the fact that it dispenses through a spray mist. This is cool because you can spray the ground, ferns, leaves, and other things without the debris sticking to the applicator. A bottle also lasts a very long time—with one bottle lasting an entire season, in theory. You'll also use it for your everyday hunting adventures as well. I recommend getting two bottles.

I use this attractant throughout the season when I'm non-scrape hunting as well because of its calming and luring effect. The Deer Dander lure can also be used the following year if you have some left over and will still smell like a deer. This saves you money because you don't have to dispose of it when the hunting season's over. If you're like me though, you'll end up using it all because it works. Spray it directly onto the scrape and around where you kicked up the dirt. Spray it on the surrounding brush, ferns, leaves and even tree trunks to really get the smell of deer throughout the area.

I chose a synthetic urine called: "BF Pre/Post Rut," from the manufacturer named Buck Fever. I tried other brands but ultimately settled on this product because it outperformed the others. The synthetic lure was picked because it doesn't degrade or dissolve for a long time in the field—rain withstanding—unlike real urine. Like the other scent/lure, it smells like every deer. It will still cook effectively without needing to be freshened up manually. The Buck Fever synthetic urine costs between eight and fifteen dollars, depending on the size you want to buy. I buy the bigger, eight ounce pre/post rut version for about $15 because I use it for everyday hunting purposes as well. I've found it to be less than half the price of conventional lures.

An added bonus is that you can use what's left over the following season because it has an unlimited shelf life. The best way to describe this lure is to liken it to ammonia. When deer urine breaks down, it gives off an ammonia-like smell. This is the lure that you squirt liberally right onto the scrape itself as if you were using real deer urine. This is the only place you put the synthetic deer urine because that's where deer naturally pee. Do NOT squirt it on trees or shrubs to increase its effectiveness because it's not natural. Deer know this!

You can do your own experiment with these two scents while you're hunting. Apply some near a trail you think deer will traverse. Deer will literally stop dead-in-their-tracks to smell these lures.

If you want to stop a buck or doe at a certain spot to line up the perfect shot, one or both of these products are highly effective in "luring" them to stop. I've seen this theory proved time and time again.

# Too much of a Good Thing

One evening I was a bit too excited and got carried away while spraying Deer Dander around my scrape before I climbed a tree. I think I sprayed every bush and shrub in the county that night. I was in my tree maybe an hour when that familiar crackling of leaves and branches came into earshot. I was sure the biggest buck in the woods was coming my way. Although hearing this beast well before spotting him should've been my tip off, it wasn't. He kept circling around me, and some time had passed before I finally got a look at him. It was none other than Wile E. Coyote himself. He slipped in and sat right down, smack dab on a log, ten yards from my mock scrape. We were both miffed; I didn't expect to see him, and he expected to hit the deer jackpot.

# To Each His Own

Every scrape you make will take on its own characteristics—with some producing bucks right away and others producing does. There are three traits that have proven standard to my technique throughout the experiments:

- First, bucks and does came to my mock scrapes even before the hunting season opened.
- Second, they all produced quality bucks for the area they were set up in, they will for you too.
- Third, quality buck activity at all scrape locations, except a very few, dramatically decreased during the rut.

But by this time, with my technique, you should've harvested a nice buck anyway. But if you haven't already harvested a nice buck, try to find the does in the hopes that a nice buck is tagging along. It stands to reason that scrape hunting isn't the best way to maximize your chances of harvesting a nice buck in your area if you're hunting during the peak of the rut. I'm not saying that it can't happen, but if your time is limited like mine, the opportunity cost is too great.

You can set up about sixty yards away from your scrape and rattle, in the hopes of a nice buck coming your way that hasn't found the right doe yet. You can also bring a deer "decoy" in and set up closer to your scrape and try to rattle one in that way also. What I'm trying to say is that your mock scrapes alone may not be enough to lure in a nice buck when the smell of estrus does are in the air during the rut. That is why you want to harvest a nice buck from your scrape before the rut.

# Spooked

Something interesting was discovered from the experiments that I'd been doing for years without realizing its negative impact. Everything in a certain mock scrape experiment was controlled and identical to the previous tests, right down to the camera. With this test, a hanging scent dripper with high-end natural doe in estrus scent instead of the Buck Fever was used. This was the same kind of dripper that we all see in the sporting goods stores. A nice buck approached the scrape during the evening shooting hours and walked up to it like usual. When he put his nose to the scent dripper, he immediately bolted as if his life depended on it. You'll see a camouflage bag hanging off the licking branch in the top, middle portion of the following pictures. There is a circular tube at the bottom of the scent dripper where the deer urine drips out. The scent dripper was hanging outside for two weeks to get rid of all human scent before this experiment began. As an added precaution, rubber gloves were worn when attaching it to the tree. Deer love the smell of Deer Dander and were actively engaged in its smell at every previous licking branch made. Therefore, the scent dripper was also sprayed with "Deer Dander" but with very different results this time.

The behavior of that buck at that site was alarming, and the footage was studied in depth. Store bought "scent drippers" have a small amount of doe urine at the end of the rubber tube waiting to drip out.

When the buck smelled that, he fled because it wasn't natural to have doe urine up in a tree. Deer pee on the ground. It was alarming.

I know it wasn't the doe urine itself that spooked him because it was a freshly opened bottle of quality estrus urine. What spooked him to the point of not returning again was the placement of the lure. It's logical to assume that if I'd used the "Buck Fever" lure, it would've had the same effect on him. Anything that smells like urine (pee) should be on the ground. If you use a scent dripper, be very careful on its placement. You have to put it high enough above an outstretched buck neck so he can't smell the residual urine. Don't use it as your licking branch either because it will be too high to reach.

The synthetic lure will clog up the scent dripper, so that won't work either. The reason for using a scent dripper is mainly because it has a time-release dispersal system that refreshes the scrape to keep the scent there. There is no reason to use a scent dripper with my method because the Buck Fever will not evaporate, even though I choose to refresh it——adding more scent every five to seven days. But if you chose to use a hanging scent dripper, keep it high off the ground and use natural urine. Synthetic urine will clog it. You can't use that as your licking branch either because it's too high. You will have to spray a lower branch with Deer Dander, one a buck can get to with his nose!

In case you're wondering how high and outstretched buck neck can reach to smell something in the air, the next few pictures illustrate just how high.

75

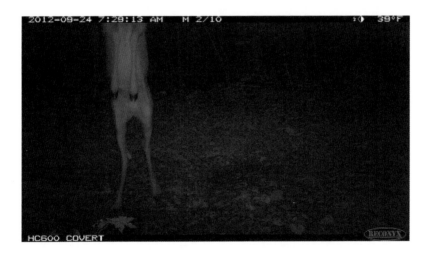

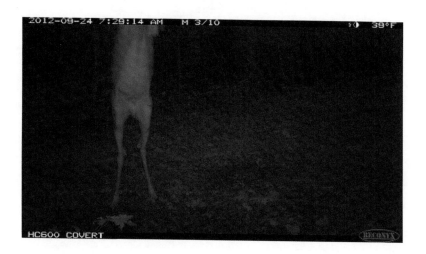

# Trail/Game Cameras

This research has shown that if things look natural, deer will act natural. Infrared and flash cameras aren't natural. Test results were gathered from inexpensive cameras to very expensive cameras. With all of the infrared and flash cameras that were placed on mock scrapes, the results were the same. They all spooked deer. There were a few pictures of bucks visiting the scrapes, but every one of them got spooked when the red or white flash went off because there weren't any more pictures after that. If you want to use one of these types of cameras, you will have to reposition it.

Fasten it higher in the tree, maybe six feet off the ground and tilt it downward. This will help keep the flash out of the buck's eyes. If you notice that it's still spooking bucks, get it out of there. Flash cameras are still a very useful tool for finding deer in your area, but they aren't best suited for placing on mock scrapes.

The camera I use is the Reconyx HC600, and none of the wonderful deer footage would've been possible without it. It truly captures deer in their natural habitat without disturbing them, as you've seen! This camera sells from $450.00 to $550.00 and is loaded with very useful features. Its flash is totally undetectable by a deer's eye and a true no flash camera. It also has the ability to continuously take pictures—as long as there's movement in its field of view—looking more like a flawless video. It has the ability to take at least two photos per second, so you don't miss anything. The footage of the buck getting spooked by the hanging scent dripper would also not have been possible without the blazing fast pictures from this camera. There were over two hundred pictures taken of that quick experiment. I'm not saying you have to purchase this camera, but it's been truly awesome for me. This camera will not spook deer even in the darkest hours of the night. If you purchase or use a camera to monitor your mock scrapes, at least make sure it's of the "no-glow" or "black-out" variety if you don't opt for the Reconyx HC 600. Even these types of non Reconyx cameras may still spook deer on scrapes at night, but they work better than traditional flash cameras. If this happens, move the camera higher and tilt it downward to limit the chances of a buck seeing the flash.

I can't watch every scrape personally, and my own human scent can spook deer. I needed a "partner" that would take pictures while I wasn't there—pictures of deer acting like deer, not like a burglar getting caught red-handed! Two infrared flash camera pictures below illustrate what happens when a buck's alarmed. I wish I'd had my Reconyx there instead because that was a nice buck—I'd love to have gotten more footage of him before he got spooked.

10/18/10  4:21 AM

Putting a game camera near a mock scrape or even a natural scrape is a tricky proposition at best. This is a very personal area in the life of a White-tailed buck. You're totally invading his privacy, like if someone put a camera in your bedroom.

10/18/10  4:22 AM

If you want to be able to pull it off, you need a camera that doesn't emit a flash. Anything else is a waste of time, and you may as well shoot yourself in the foot. There are still many brands of these cameras that emit a small amount of game spooking flash. If you see this happening, try moving it higher and tilt it downward.

If you don't want to bother with using a camera to see the caliber of bucks living in your hunting area, don't use one. Trust there's at least one nice buck visiting your scrape, and harvest him!

Your hunting adventures will be forever changed. I guarantee you'll see many more bucks than ever before and be hooked on this

81

technique also. Make some space on the wall and in the photo album because you're going to have some amazing memories to share with your hunting buddies and loved ones. Of course you'll be chomping at the bit to go scouting even earlier every year now—you'll soon know just what's sniffing around in your deer woods. I would absolutely love to see your amazing camera footage and hear your stories. Feel free to add me on facebook under Gale Bott in Marquette, MI. You can also email me at: gbottman@gmail.com.

Thank you for reading my research. You will have a more enjoyable and productive time in the woods this and every hunting season to come.

*I was not paid by any manufacturer for my research, nor was I given any promotional products.

43071698R00052

Made in the USA
Lexington, KY
16 July 2015